W9-AHY-758

HUMPBACK GOES NORTH

SMITHSONIAN OCEANIC COLLECTION

To my brothers and sisters —
Alben, Ferne, Stafford, Benson, Julian, Jackie, and Jeremy.
  — D. B.

Dedicated to Christine and Alexander.
  — S.M.

Book copyright © 1998 Trudy Corporation, 353 Main Avenue, Norwalk, CT 06851,
and the Smithsonian Institution, Washington, DC 20560.

Soundprints is a division of Trudy Corporation, Norwalk, Connecticut.

All rights reserved. No part of this book may be reproduced or transmitted in any form or by any means
whatsoever without prior written permission of the publisher.

Book Design: Diane Hinze Kanzler

First Edition 1998
10 9 8 7 6 5 4 3 2 1
Printed in Singapore

Acknowledgements:
  Our very special thanks to Dr. Charles Handley of the Department of Vertebrate Zoology
at the Smithsonian Institution's National Museum of Natural History for his curatorial review.

Library of Congress Cataloging-in-Publication Data

Bailer, Darice.

  Humpback goes north / by Darice Bailer ; illustrated by Stephen Marchesi.
      p.   cm.
  Summary: When Little Whale makes her first migration to the north, she and her mother
  have some narrow escapes.
      ISBN 1-56899-525-3
  [1. Whales — Fiction.   2. Mothers and daughters — Fiction.]
  I. Marchesi, Stephen, ill.   II. Title.
      PZ7.B1447Hu 1998   97-47615
      [E] — dc21   CIP
                                                            AC

HUMPBACK GOES NORTH

by *Darice Bailer*   Illustrated by *Stephen Marchesi*

One April morning, a baby humpback whale and her mother rise to the surface of the aqua-colored ocean where the Atlantic joins the Caribbean Sea. Little Whale is one month old, and is beginning her first journey.

Each spring, Little Whale's mother migrates to Maine, to find the small fish that live in the north Atlantic. She eats nothing all winter, and now she is very hungry.

Little Whale follows her mother away from Navidad Bank, where she was born in a warm patch of ocean north of the Dominican Republic. They must swim thirty to sixty miles each day, stopping only to nurse or rest.

Arching her back, Little Whale dives. She nuzzles against her mother's belly, feeding from nipples tucked into slits in her mother's skin. She gulps down milk that is as thick as heavy cream.

Soon, Little Whale comes back up to the surface to breathe. She can only stay under water for five minutes at a time. Her mother can stay down for up to forty minutes, but Little Whale's lungs are still small.

She exhales through the two blow-holes on top of her head, and sends moist air six feet high. Her mother surfaces alongside her and blasts a misty plume of spray more than ten feet into the air!

Using her huge flippers, Little Whale turns onto her back, showing the deep grooves running from her chin to her belly button. She waves the flippers in the air and does a backward dive.

Under water, Little Whale hears strange sounds coming through the ocean. *Ooreek! Ooreek!* The musical sounds come from a male humpback, floating head down in the water and blowing air from his throat. The unusual noises form a beautiful song.

This humpback bull is singing to attract female humpbacks. He hopes a cow will answer, and swim closer so that they can mate.

Little Whale's mother ignores him. She strokes Little Whale with her flippers, nudging her baby on, eager to continue their journey northward. Little Whale flips back onto her belly and follows her mother.

After a while, Little Whale's mother slows.
Barnacles on her skin are bothering her, and she
is going to do something about it. She lowers her head,
arches her back, and dives. Her flukes—large, fan-like fins
on the end of her tail—disappear under the water.
    Suddenly, Little Whale's mother zooms toward the sky.
Halfway out of the water, she swings her flippers and twists.
When her whole body is out of the water, she hangs in mid-air!

But only for an instant! Then, she crashes down
on her back on the surface of the ocean. That will
knock off some of the bothersome barnacles! Fountains
of water spray up around her, making waves that bounce
Little Whale around.

Little Whale wants to copy her mother.
She dives, but jumps only halfway out
of the water, smacking her grooved throat
instead of her back. Swimming over,
she playfully lies across her mother's head,
but gets shaken off. Her mother cannot
breathe if Little Whale covers her blowholes!

17

That night, Little Whale and her mother stop to rest off the coast of Georgia. They float in the calm water. A sliver of moon barely lights the sky. Suddenly, Little Whale hears and feels the water vibrating. Waves lap at her, rocking her from side to side. Little Whale looks toward the sound, and sees the sharp-edged bow of a coast-guard cutter racing toward her.

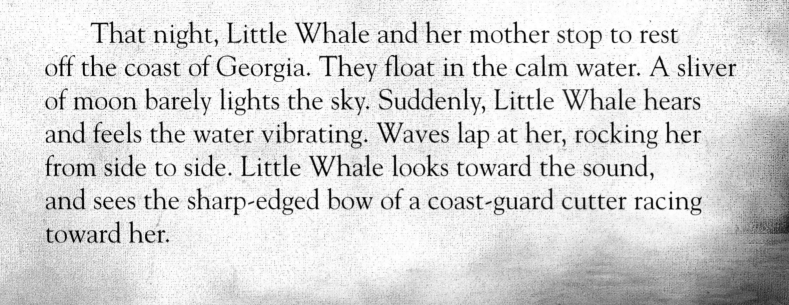

It is dark. The cutter's pilot cannot see
Little Whale and her mother in the water.
If the boat hits them, it will tear into their skin.
It might even kill them. Little Whale's mother
swoops in front of her baby to protect her.
Luckily, the cutter passes by without harming them.
It roars out of sight as Little Whale peers around her mother.
The choppy waves subside. The danger has passed.

Next morning, Little Whale again feels vibrations in the water. This time, she sees something churning slowly nearby. It is not moving as fast as the cutter.

Curious, Little Whale pokes her snout up twenty feet away from a cruise ship on its way to Bermuda. Little Whale's mother surfaces between Little Whale and the ship and nudges her baby to a safe distance.

After swimming for about five weeks, Little Whale and her mother finally reach the coast of Maine. They join a group of humpbacks who will all spend the summer there. Little Whale has completed her first journey north!

Now, there is more time to play. As her mother rises up for air, Little Whale swims onto her mother's back. When her mother gets to the surface, Little Whale slides down her mother's back and zips off her tail flukes, splashing into the water.

Diving down, Little Whale sees thousands of krill darting around. They are her mother's favorite food. At the surface, Little Whale's mother smashes her tail flukes against the water and dives. Little Whale sees her swim down beneath the krill, joined by two other humpbacks. They all blow bubbles from their blowholes that rise up and circle the krill and other fish in a "bubble net."

Little Whale watches the three big whales swoop through the center of the bubble net. With their mouths wide open they swim upward, scooping gallons of water, and hundreds of fish and krill, into their mouths. Their throats bulge! The baleen hanging from their upper jaws hold the fish and krill inside, while the humpbacks push the cold sea water out with their huge tongues.

After Little Whale's mother fills her belly, she begins to play, too. With her head down and her tail poking up, she slaps the water with her flukes, first in front of her, then in back. Water splashes all around! Little Whale tries, but she can't make much of a splash yet. She must nurse and grow for at least a year more.

Little Whale's first day in Maine is coming to an end. The sky is royal blue and the lowering sun is gold, but Little Whale doesn't want to rest yet. She is too busy playing in the deep green ocean, safely at her mother's side.

About the Humpback Whale

Humpback whales are found in every ocean of the world. They are dark gray or black, with different white markings on their flippers, bellies, or tail flukes that can identify each whale like a fingerprint. They can grow to be sixty feet long and have longer flippers than any other whale.

A humpback has about twenty-five tube-shaped grooves along its belly that stretch out like a bag when the whale feeds, gulping gallons of water with its food. Instead of teeth, a humpback has about 125 blade-shaped baleen, or "whalebones," hanging from its upper jaw that strain the food out of the water.

From January through March they live in warm, tropical waters, where they breed and give birth. They migrate more than 1,500 miles to northern feeding waters in the spring. Grown humpbacks will follow the same route they traveled as calves.

In 1985 there were only about 7,000 humpbacks left in the whole world. Now they are protected by the International Whaling Commission, and the number has grown to 50,000. These whales are not shy and are often seen on whale watches.

Glossary

baleen: blades of horn-like whalebone hanging from a whale's upper jaw. The frayed inner edges trap food and filter out water.

barnacles: small shellfish that attach to the sides of boats, rocks, and large sea creatures.

blowholes: two nostril openings on top of a humpback's head through which the whale breathes. They open when the whale is above water, and close when it dives.

cutter: an armed, high-speed motorboat used by the Coast Guard.

flippers: paddle-like limbs on the humpback's sides that help it steer and swim.

flukes: wide, fan-like fins at the end of a humpback's strong tail. By moving the flukes up and down the whale pushes itself through the water.

krill: small, shrimp-like sea animals that swim in shallow water.

migrate: to move from one region to another at certain seasons each year.

vibrations: quick back and forth movements that may be heard, seen, or felt.

Points of Interest in this Book

pp. 4-5 a whale calf swims just above its mother, always on a favorite side.

pp. 8-9 the blowhole is the "nose" of a whale. "Lips" close over it when the whale is under water, and open when it surfaces to breathe.

pp. 10-11 humpback's flippers average about one-third of the total length of the whale.

pp. 14-15 white markings on flukes are different on each whale, like fingerprints on a person.

pp. 16-17 humpbacks are playful and acrobatic and are the champion breachers (jumpers) of all whales.

pp. 28-29 the whale's grooved throat spreads out like a bag when it takes in water and food.